FAMOUS PEOPLE
FAMOUS LIVES

Biographies of famous people to
support the curriculum.

Boudicca

by Emma Fischel

Illustrations by Peter Chesterton

First published in 2000
by Franklin Watts
This edition 2002

Franklin Watts
96 Leonard Street
London EC2A 4XD

Franklin Watts Australia
56 O'Riordan Street
Alexandria, Sydney
NSW 2015

© 2000 text Emma Fischel
© 2000 illustrations Peter Chesterton

The right of the author to be identified as the author of this work has been asserted.

The right of the illustrator to be identified as the illustrator of this work has been asserted.

ISBN 0 7496 4361 7 (pbk)

A CIP catalogue record for this book is available from the British Library

Dewey Decimal Classification
Number: 942.01

10 9 8 7 6 5 4 3 2 1

Series Editor: Sarah Ridley
Historical Consultant: Barbara Searle

Printed in Great Britain

Boudicca

Two thousand years ago Britain was a wild, war-like place. Fierce groups of people, belonging to tribes, fought each other to the death. Bears and wolves roamed the forests ...

and baby Boudicca was born.

The people of that time were known as the Celts.

The Celts had come from many different places to live in Britain. They were all brave, proud warriors.

Little Boudicca would grow up
to be one of the bravest warriors
of them all.

The Celts were divided into lots of separate tribes. They often fought terrible and bloody battles with each other for food or land.

From early on Boudicca learned all about the tribe she belonged to, the Iceni.

There was no reading or writing,
and no books then, so stories of
brave deeds were passed on
from older to younger men in
the tribe.

7

Anything the Iceni tribe wanted,
they had to grow or make.
Mostly they made useful things,

like pots or clothes, but they also made beautiful jewellery and weapons from metal.

Most people lived in simple thatched huts. They cooked, ate and slept all in one room.

Boudicca was probably from a noble family. But even nobles slept on raised banks of earth, like benches, in the huts.

By the time Boudicca was grown up, she had married the most important person in the whole Iceni tribe, King Prasutagus.

Soon they had a baby daughter, and then another one.

But these were dangerous times to live in. Boudicca knew there was something to be feared even more than attack by other tribes ... the Roman army.

The Roman army was the most powerful in the world.

"Invade and conquer!" the Roman leaders ordered their army time and time again. "Rome must rule the world!"

While Boudicca was growing up the Romans arrived in Britain.

The Celts fought hard but it was no use. One by one the tribes were beaten.

By the time Boudicca was married, the Romans ruled over the Iceni and many other tribes.

King Prasutagus decided to make a sort of agreement with the Romans.

But many Iceni warriors thought
that was a terrible thing to do.

"Peace is the best plan," said
Prasutagus. "No army of ours
can EVER defeat these Romans!"

Time passed and Boudicca
watched her daughters grow
taller and stronger every year.

But King Prasutagus was growing weaker and weaker.

May the peace with Rome continue after my death.

In the end, he died.

"Our king is dead," said Boudicca. "Now I shall rule the Iceni in the name of my daughters, the heirs to the throne. I shall keep our tribe strong."

But back then, the Romans didn't think a woman COULD be a strong leader.

"This Boudicca," they said. "How can SHE lead the tribe? And her daughters become rulers in their turn? What nonsense!"

There was worse to come.
Prasutagus had made a secret
will before his death. He hoped
it would keep peace for the tribe.

"King Prasutagus leaves half his
kingdom to Emperor Nero of
Rome!" announced the Romans.

But half a kingdom wasn't
enough for the Romans.

"We shall take it all!" they said.

The Romans attacked Boudicca's home. Anything they wanted, they took.

Then they turned their attention to Boudicca and her daughters.

"Beat them, mistreat them, then throw them all out!" said the Roman leaders. "No need to kill them, not even the queen. She can do nothing against us!"

And THAT was their big mistake.

Now Boudicca knew what she must do.

"Death to those who harm my daughters!" she said. "Suffering to those who humiliate the Iceni tribe and their queen!"

"I, Boudicca, warrior queen, will gather all the tribes to join me! We will fight as one against Rome!"

"We are fierce! We are strong! We are cunning! We know our land, our hills and forests! We CAN defeat them!"

The Romans weren't worried by fears of rebellion.

"What use are painted faces and fierce war cries against the best trained army in the world?" they said.

"Besides, those savages can't stop fighting each other. No one, woman OR man, can bring them together to fight us!"

But Boudicca could. Tribe after
tribe was streaming to join her.

"Forget old quarrels," Boudicca
urged them all. "Our enemy is
not each other. Take up your
weapons and unite against
Rome!"

"They have strong armour but we have right on our side. They have mighty weapons but we have revenge in our hearts!"

Boudicca and her army surged into the most important Roman town of all, Camulodonum.

"Freedom from Rome!" cried Boudicca. Then they struck.

The Romans had no chance. "This woman and her wild army are destroying our town. Send in more troops," they begged their leaders.

But Boudicca was ready for those troops too.

Within days the whole town was destroyed. Thousands of Romans died in the blazing ruins, or were hacked to pieces as they tried to escape.

"Onwards!" cried Boudicca to her army. "Camulodonum is gone! Now for Londinium!"

Boudicca and her army
marched onwards, first to
Londinium, and then to
Verulamium. They killed,

looted and destroyed. Men, women and children were all slaughtered without mercy. Nothing could stop them now.

Even other Celts, from tribes who supported Rome, were doomed.

"This woman will kill or drive out every Roman in Britain," said the Romans. "She has ruined our proudest achievements, our greatest towns. We MUST destroy her!"

North of Verulamium, the Romans gathered more and more troops together.

But now the Romans were ready for battle. Their army was in place, and they had chosen the battle site carefully.

"Northwards!" said Boudicca to her army. "And hurry! Every hour we delay, the Roman army grows bigger!"

Those who couldn't fight were
gathered to watch the victory.

"Forwards!" cried Boudicca.
And so the last battle began.

This time the Romans made no
mistakes. In a few short hours
thousands of Celts were dead.
The rest had no way to escape.

They were surrounded by the
Roman cavalry and trapped
by their own carts behind them.
It was over.

Boudicca tried to surrender to save the lives of her people.

"No surrender," said the Romans.

"It is the end," said Boudicca.
"My land and people will never
be free."

But Boudicca was not going to
let the Romans take her alive.
She put a bottle of poison to her
lips... then she drank.

Further facts

More about the Celts

The Celts did not write anything about themselves, so we have to find out about them in other ways.

Many things from Celtic times have been found buried in the ground. Archaeologists can tell a lot about the Celts from studying them.

They know that the Celts believed that after someone died, life went on in the Otherworld. Archaeologists have found remains of Celts buried with things they might need there – food, weapons, necklaces, even games!

The Otherworld was the home of the Celtic gods and a very happy place. Everyone went there, whether they had been good or bad. However, if you were poor, your body would be buried with nothing to help you on your journey to the Otherworld.

The Romans wrote about the way the Celts lived. One Roman tells us about a 'belt tax'. Any warrior who got too fat to do up his belt was fined!

Some important dates in Boudicca's lifetime

We do not know the exact dates of events in Boudicca's life but we do know the order in which they happened.

c35-40 Boudicca is born in the Iceni tribe.

55 The Romans invade Britain. Boudicca marries the king of the tribe, Prasutagus. They have two daughters.

c60 Prasutagus dies and Boudicca becomes leader of the Iceni.

c61 The Romans seize Boudicca's home and throw her family out. Boudicca gathers an army and marches on Camulodonum (now Colchester) and destroys it. The army does the same in Londinium (now London) and Verulamium (now St Albans).

c62 Boudicca and her army are defeated and Boudicca dies. Huge numbers of the Iceni tribe die in the fighting and afterwards, when the Romans take terrible revenge on them.